The Funny Side of Parenthood

The Best Quotes, Quips, & Rhymes

Selected by **Bruce Lansky**

Meadowbrook Press
Distributed by Simon & Schuster
New York, NY

Library of Congress Cataloging-in-Publication Data

The Funny side of parenthood : the best quotes, quips, and rhymes / selected
by Bruce Lansky.
    p.   cm.
  1. Parenting—Humor.   2.   Parenting—Quotations, maxims, etc.
  3. Child rearing—Humor.   4.   Child rearing—Quotations, maxims, etc.
  I. Lansky, Bruce.
  PN6231.P2F86   1994
  818'.540208—dc20   93–40520
                                                            CIP

ISBN 0-88166-206-2

Simon & Schuster Ordering # 0-671-88444-1

Managing Editor: Dale Howard
Assistant Editor: Cathy Broberg
Production Manager: Amy Unger
Desktop Publishing Manager: Jon C. Wright

Copyright © 1994 by Meadowbrook Creations

Published by Meadowbrook Press, 18318 Minnetonka Boulevard, Deephaven,
MN 55391.

BOOK TRADE DISTRIBUTION by Simon & Schuster, a division of Simon and
Schuster, Inc., 1230 Avenue of the Americas, New York, NY 10020.

99 98 97 96 95 94 10 9 8 7 6 5 4 3 2 1

Printed in the United States of America.

Acknowledgments:

NOTICE: Every effort has been made to locate the copyright owners of the material used in this book. Please let us know of any errors, and we will gladly make any necessary corrections in subsequent printings.

We would like to thank the people who served on our "humor panel": Polly Anderson, Jim Bohen, Phil Bolsta, Chris Bruce, Larry Cohen, Eileen Daily, Linda Fiterman, Charles Ghigna, Babs Bell Hajdusiewicz, Jo S. Kittinger, Sydnie Meltzer Kleinhenz, Kim Koehler, Lois Muehl, Robert Scotellaro, Linda Torres, Penny Warner, David Wexler, and Steve Zweig.

We would also like to thank the photographers and writers who contributed material used in this book.

Photographs: p. 42 © Suzanne Arms/Jeroboam, Inc.; p. 39 © 1960 by Bill Binzen; pp. 61 © Ralph Bouton, Greenville, SC; p. 75 © Ed Buryn/Jeroboam, Inc.; pp. 47 and 102 © 1993 by Elizabeth Harburg; p. 80 © Michal Heron/ Woodfin Camp; p. 89 "Teenage Girl w/ Green Facial Mask" © 1991 by Ken Lax; p. vi © Kent Reno/Jeroboam, Inc.; p. 93 © Jim Richardson/West Light; pp. 3, 9, and 28 © H. Armstrong Roberts; p. 12 © 1978 Schieffelin & Somerset Co., formerly Somerset Importers, Ltd.; p. 17 © Kathy Sloane/Jeroboam, Inc.; pp. 6, 22, 35, 52, 56, and 65 © by Wide World Photos; pp. 68 and 97 © Bob Willoughby 1993.

Poem: p. 37 "The Parent" by Ogden Nash. From *Verses from 1929 On* by Ogden Nash. Copyright 1931, 1933 by Ogden Nash. By permission of Little Brown and Company. Reprinted by permission of Curtis Brown, Ltd. Copyright 1933 by Ogden Nash.

Dedication

I set out to publish the funniest quotes, quips, and rhymes about parenthood ever written or spoken. So, I submitted the very best entries I could find from best-selling authors, famous stand-up comics, celebrity quipsters, wits and wags, renowned rhymsters, as well as relative unknowns in all categories, to a "humor panel." And, I made all my selections based on the panel's objective ratings.

As a result of this process, I gained the greatest respect for two humorists whose quotes consistently rated higher than any others tested. And so I dedicate this book to the "king" and "queen" of parenthood humor: Mark Twain and Erma Bombeck.

I also want to salute two relative newcomers: Babs Bell Hajdusiewicz and Linda Fiterman. Their quotes and rhymes compare favorably with their better-known peers. It is a pleasure both to recognize the quality of the very best humorists and to discover bright new ones.

I hope this book brings the gift of laughter to parents world wide. If I've missed some side-splitting quotes, quips, or rhymes, please mail them to me (in care of Meadowbrook Press) so I can include them in a later edition of this book.

Bruce Lansky

Contents

Introduction

If you read child-care manuals and magazines, you probably come up with laundry lists of things you don't do "right" and even more lists of things that could go "wrong" as a result.

Take consistency, for example. Try as you may to be consistent in your parenting style, your kids still figure out exactly what it takes to make you angry. Consistently.

Looking at parenthood from a humorous point of view reinforces a more realistic perspective. Reading quotes by humorists like Mark Twain, Dave Barry, and Erma Bombeck; TV personalities like Bill Cosby and Roseanne Arnold; and stand-up comics like Steven Wright and Rita Rudner is a terrific antidote to child-care manuals.

I sifted through thousands of quotes and rhymes to come up with the gems of wit and wisdom in this book. (About 20 experienced parents helped me make the final selection.) I wanted to collect the most entertaining and illuminating quotes about parenthood ever published in a single book. I visualized a book that would help expectant parents gain a realistic view of what's ahead and let accomplished parents know that they did not struggle alone—all through laughter.

Parenthood really is a joyful experience, especially when you finally realize that it's not supposed to be easy—that mistakes are par for the course. After all, parenthood is an unpaid job that puts you "on-call" 24 hours a day. It's definitely not a job for wimps.

Bruce Lansky

Nurses nurse
and teachers teach
and tailors mend
and preachers preach
and barbers trim
and chauffeurs haul
and parents get to do it all.

—Babs Bell Hajdusiewicz

Familiarity breeds children.

—*Mark Twain*

Parenthood is a lot easier to get into
than out of.

—*Bruce Lansky*

If your parents never had children,
chances are you won't, either.

—*Dick Cavett*

A crying baby is the best form of
birth control.

—*Carole Tabbron*

Have children while your parents are still
young enough to take care of them.

—*Rita Rudner*

An advantage to having one child is
you always know who did it.

—*Babs Bell Hajdusiewicz*

I came from a big family.
As a matter of fact, I never got to sleep alone
until I was married.

—*Lewis Grizzard*

It goes without saying that you should never have more children than you have car windows.

—*Erma Bombeck*

God could not be everywhere. That's why he made mothers.

—*Jewish Proverb*

If evolution really works, how come mothers only have two hands?

—*Milton Berle*

It's not easy being a mother. If it were easy, fathers would do it.

—*Dorothy on* The Golden Girls

Hey, the way I figure it is this: if the kids are still alive by the time my husband comes home, I've done my job.

—*Roseanne Arnold*

Any mother could perform the jobs of several air traffic controllers with ease.

—*Lisa Alther*

The phrase "working mother" is redundant.

—*Jane Sellman*

Any man can be a father. It takes someone special to be a dad.

—Poster

When I meet a man I ask myself, "Is this the man I want my children to spend their weekends with?"

—Rita Rudner

I never got along with my dad. Kids used to come up to me and say, "My dad can beat up your dad." I'd say, "Yeah? When?"

—Bill Hicks

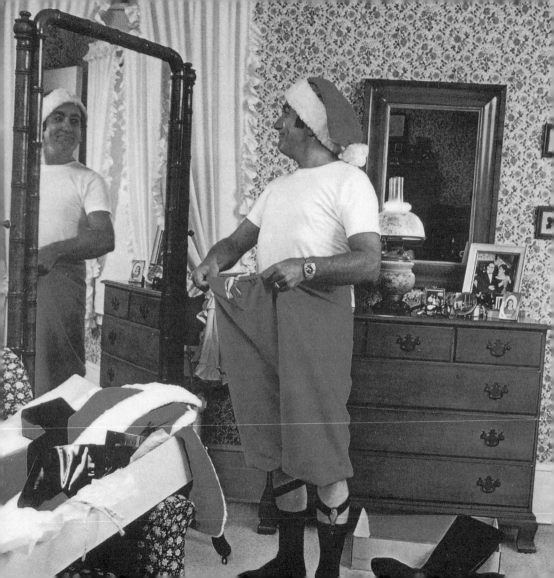

There are three stages of a man's life:

1. He believes in Santa Claus.
2. He doesn't believe in Santa Claus.
3. He is Santa Claus.

—Anonymous

I feel really lucky that my children have inherited all of my good traits: looks, charm, wisdom, and objectivity.

—*Robert Scotellaro*

We modern, sensitive husbands realize that it's very unfair to place the entire child-care burden on our wives, so many of us are starting to assume maybe three percent of it.

—*Dave Barry*

Prepared childbirth is
a contradiction in terms.

—Joyce Armor

Childbirth classes neglect to teach one
critical skill: How to breathe, count, and
swear all at the same time.

—Linda Fiterman

I already know how to breathe, and I'm the
last person that needs to learn how to push.

—Murphy Brown on Murphy Brown

Life is tough enough without having someone kick you from the inside.

—Rita Rudner

In my last stage of labor I threatened to take my husband to court for concealing a lethal weapon in his boxer shorts.

—*Linda Fiterman*

I'd be happy to stand next to any man I know in one of those labor rooms the size of a Volkswagen trunk and whisper, "No dear, you don't really need the Demerol; just relax and do your second-stage breathing."

—*Anna Quindlen*

Having a baby is like taking your bottom lip
and pulling it over your head.

—*Carol Burnett*

Have you ever tried to get out of your car
through the exhaust pipe?

—*Murphy Brown on* Murphy Brown

If men had babies, maternity leave would be
in the Bill of Rights.

—*Corky Sherwood Forest on* Murphy Brown

. . . as they started to clean it off . . . I went over to my wife, kissed her gently on the lips, and said, "Darling, I love you very much. You just had a lizard."

—*Bill Cosby*

I was cesarean born. You can't really tell, although whenever I leave a house, I go out through a window.

—*Steven Wright*

CONGRATS! We all knew you had it in you!

—*Dorothy Parker*

Think of stretch marks as pregnancy service stripes.

—*Joyce Armor*

People said I'd slim down quickly. Nobody told me it was because I'd never have time to eat.

—*Anonymous*

21

His mother's eyes,
His father's chin,
His auntie's nose,
His uncle's grin,

His great-aunt's hair,
His grandma's ears,
His grandpa's mouth,
So it appears . . .

Poor little tot,
Well may he moan.
He hasn't much
To call his own.

—Richard Armour

When I was born I was so surprised I didn't talk for a year and a half.

—*Gracie Allen*

Now why did you name your baby John? Every Tom, Dick, or Harry is named John.

—*Samuel Goldwyn*

My wife wanted to call our daughter Sue, but I felt that in our family that was usually a verb.

—*Dennis Wolfberg*

A soiled baby with a neglected nose
cannot be conscientiously regarded as
a thing of beauty.

> —*Mark Twain*

Men who have fought in the world's
bloodiest wars . . . are apt to faint at the
sight of a truly foul diaper.

> —*Gary D. Christenson*

One of the most important things
to remember about infant care is: never
change diapers in midstream.

—Don Marquis

Babies leak. From both ends.

—Bruce Lansky

First-time parents never miss
    a single tiny feat.
They film it, note it in The Book,
    and shout it in the street:
"He smiled today! Had four BMs!
    He spit up on the cat!
He got a tooth! He slept all night—
    can you imagine that?"

But second-timers note the facts
    and take each one in stride:
"He's learned to take his diaper off—
    you'd better step aside."

—Babs Bell Hajdusiewicz

27

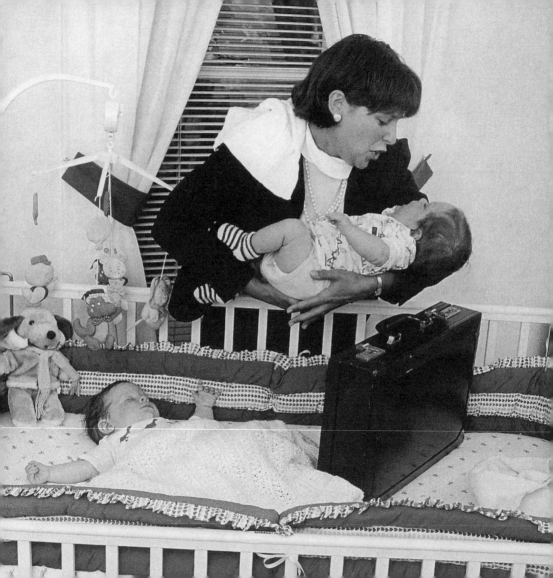

Taking care of a baby is easy—if you
have nothing else to do.

—Bruce Lansky

People who say they sleep like babies
usually don't have them.

—*Leo J. Burke*

You know that having a baby has drastically
changed your life when you and your
husband go on a date to Wal-Mart on double
coupon day.

—*Linda Fiterman*

I always wondered why babies spend
so much time sucking their thumbs.
Then I tasted baby food.

—Robert Orben

If you think it's easy to take candy away
from a baby—you should try it.

—Henny Youngman

When your first baby drops her
pacifier, you sterilize it. When your
second baby drops her pacifier, you
tell the dog: "Fetch."

—Bruce Lansky

Whatever is on the floor
will wind up in your baby's mouth.
Whatever is in your baby's mouth
will wind up on the floor.

—Bruce Lansky

One of the great ironies . . . is that feeding children, a task whose misery cannot be overstated, leads to more diaper changing.

—*Gary D. Christenson*

Toddlers are more likely to eat healthy food if they find it on the floor.

—*Jan Blaustone*

There are hundreds of different toilet-training methods—probably because none of them work.

—*Bruce Lansky*

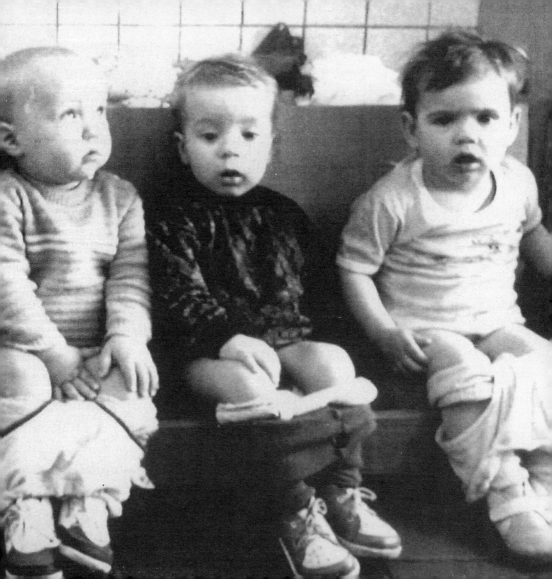

Reasoning with a two-year-old is about as productive as changing seats on the *Titanic.*

—*Robert Scotellaro*

Don't tell your two-year-old she's driving you nuts. She just might say, "Mama nuts," to everyone she meets.

—*Jan Blaustone*

Nothing brings out a toddler's devotion to a toy she has abandoned more quickly than another child playing with it.

—*Robert Scotellaro*

What is a home without children? Quiet.

> —*Henny Youngman*

Children aren't happy with nothing to ignore. And that's what parents were created for.

> —*Ogden Nash*

Children are unpredictable. You never know what inconsistency they're going to catch you in next.

> —*Franklin P. Jones*

A child is someone who stands halfway between an adult and a TV set.

—*Anonymous*

No matter what the critics say, it's hard to believe that a television program which keeps four children quiet for an hour can be all bad.

—*Beryl Pfizer*

Adults are always asking children what they want to be when they grow up— they're looking for ideas.

—Paula Poundstone

Any kid will run any errand for you if you ask at bedtime.

—Red Skelton

When I was younger, I could remember anything, whether it happened or not.

—*Mark Twain*

When I was a girl I only had two friends, and they were imaginary. And they would only play with each other.

—*Rita Rudner*

I've got two wonderful children—and two out of five isn't too bad.

—*Henny Youngman*

41

I have seen my kid struggle into the
kitchen in the morning with outfits
that need only one accessory:
an empty gin bottle.

—Erma Bombeck

She's stubborn, contrary, and willful.
She'll grumble; she'll whine, and
    complain.
Her habits are terribly awfully smug.
Her actions are far from humane.

She's selfishly stingy and rotten.
She's lazily sluggish and slow.
Her manners are cleverly cunningly
    coy . . . but . . .
no sweeter daughter I know.

              —*Babs Bell Hajdusiewicz*

In general, my children refused to eat anything that hadn't danced on TV.

—*Erma Bombeck*

As a child, my family's menu consisted of two choices: take it or leave it.

—*Buddy Hackett*

Ask your child what he wants for dinner only if he is buying.

—*Fran Lebowitz*

Even when freshly washed
and relieved of all obvious confections,
children tend to be sticky.

—*Fran Lebowitz*

The secret to feeding your child is learning how to disguise a vegetable as a french fry.

—Jan Blaustone

The best way to prevent your children from eating fatty, greasy, disgusting, unhealthy food is: don't let them eat from your plate.

—Bill Dodds

The main reason kids eat supper is to get dessert. But the better dessert is, the less supper they eat.

—Bruce Lansky

A baby-sitter is a teenager who gets two dollars an hour to eat five dollars' worth of your food.

—*Henny Youngman*

The highlight of my childhood was making my brother laugh so hard that food came out of his nose.

—*Garrison Keillor*

A family
is a unit
composed not only of children
but of men,
women,
an occasional animal
and the common cold.

—*Ogden Nash*

If you can't open a childproof bottle,
use pliers or ask your child.

—*Bruce Lansky*

A cavity is a tiny hole in your child's tooth
that takes many, many dollars to fill.

—*Bill Dodds*

The only way to make sure your child goes
to the dentist is to schedule the appointment
during school hours.

—*Bruce Lansky*

My kids would never share anything of
their own free will—except germs.

—*Bruce Lansky*

How do you explain "counterclockwise" to a child with a digital watch?

—*Anonymous*

There's a time when you have to explain
to your children why they're born,
and it's a marvelous thing if you know
the reason by then.

—*Hazel Scott*

We've been having some trouble with the school bus. It keeps bringing the kids back.

—*Bruce Lansky*

The reason you want your kids to pay attention in school is you haven't the faintest idea how to do their homework.

—*Babs Bell Hajdusiewicz*

Labor Day is a glorious holiday because your child will be going back to school the next day. It would have been called Independence Day, but that name was already taken.

—*Bill Dodds*

One of the disadvantages of enrolling
your daughters in dance class is that
eventually they put on a recital you
have to attend.

—Bruce Lansky

If you must give your child lessons,
send him to driving school.
He is far more likely to end up owning
a Datsun than he is a Stradivarius.

—Fran Lebowitz

I taught my child the value of a dollar.
This week he wants his allowance
in yen.

—Milton Berle

Birthday parties are a lot like childbirth. After both events you solemnly swear you'll never make that mistake again.

—*Linda Fiterman*

By the time you talk your child into writing a thank-you note for a birthday gift, it's already broken.

—*Bruce Lansky*

Do not, on a rainy day, ask your child what he feels like doing, because I assure you that what he feels like doing, you won't feel like watching.

—*Fran Lebowitz*

There is no such thing
as fun for the whole family.

—*Jerry Seinfeld on* Seinfeld

It costs more now to amuse a child than it
used to cost to educate his father.

—*Anonymous*

Why take your kids to Disneyland when for
the same money you can put them
through college?

—*Bruce Lansky*

The dough we spent on Disney World
we could have saved instead;
the ride the kids remember most
was jumping on the bed.

—*Charles Ghigna*

I take my children everywhere;
but they always find their way back home.

—*Robert Orben*

If you want to bring your family closer
together, buy a smaller car.

—*Anonymous*

There are two classes of travel—first class,
and with children.

—*Robert Benchley*

Thank goodness for the pickle jar,
   a standard feature in our car.
When sons have signaled they must go,
   and traffic's jammed or lights are slow,
our handy-dandy pickle jar
   relieves the tension where we are.
I can't imagine what folks do
   when daughters need to potty, too.

—Sydnie Meltzer Kleinhenz

Your kids will feed their new puppy
the day you buy it and the days you threaten
to take it back to the pet store.

—Bruce Lansky

If you wonder where your child left
his roller skates, try walking around the
house in the dark.

—Leopold Fechtner

Children make the most desirable
opponents in Scrabble as they are both
easy to beat and fun to cheat.

—Fran Lebowitz

Dear God, I pray for patience.
And I want it right now.

—*Oren Arnold*

We learn many things from children.
Patience, for instance.

—*Franklin P. Jones*

A child enters your home and for the next
twenty years makes so much noise you
can hardly stand it. The child departs,
leaving the house so silent you think you
are going mad.

—*John Andrew Holmes*

Insanity is hereditary—
you get it from your kids.

—*Sam Levinson*

You know you've lost control when you're
the one who goes to your room.

—*Babs Bell Hajdusiewicz*

Before I had kids I went home after work
to rest. Now I go to work to rest.

—*Simon Ruddell*

Cleaning your house while your kids are still growing is like shoveling the walk before it stops snowing.

—*Phyllis Diller*

Children are a great comfort in your old age—and they help you reach it faster, too.

—*Lionel Kauffman*

You know you've spent too much time
carpooling your kids when fast-food, drive-
through servers recognize your voice.

—*Linda Fiterman*

I was doing the family grocery shopping
accompanied by two children, an event
I hope to see included in the Olympics in
the near future.

—*Anna Quindlen*

Before I was married I had six theories about raising children. Now I have six children and no theories.

—*John Wilmot, Earl of Rochester*

Most parents find it very hard to be consistent—except when it comes to losing their temper.

—*Bruce Lansky*

I didn't make the same mistakes my parents made when they raised me. I was too busy making new ones.

—*Bruce Lansky*

The quickest way for a parent to get a child's attention is to sit down and look comfortable.

—*Lane Olinghouse*

Setting a good example for children takes all
the fun out of middle age.

—*William Feather*

Parents: A peculiar group who first try to get
their children to walk and talk, and then try
to get them to sit down and shut up.

—Wagster's *Dictionary of Humor and Wit*

When I was a kid my parents moved a lot—
but I always found them.

—*Rodney Dangerfield*

Children today are tyrants. They contradict their parents, gobble their food, and tyrannize their teachers.

—Socrates

A tornado touched down, uprooting a large tree in the front yard and demolishing the house across the street. Dad went to the door, opened it, surveyed the damage, and muttered, "Darned kids...."

—Tim Conway

The thing that impresses me most about America is the way parents obey their children.

—King Edward VII

77

Heredity is what a man believes in until his son begins to behave like a delinquent.

—*Presbyterian Life*

Children behave best when their stomachs are full and their bladders are empty.

—*Vicki Lansky*

A baby-sitter is a teenage girl you hire to let your children do whatever they want.

—*Henny Youngman*

When my kids become wild and unruly, I use a nice, safe playpen. When they're finished, I climb out.

—*Erma Bombeck*

If scientists can put a man on the moon, why can't they figure out which kid hit the other first?

—*Bruce Lansky*

Parents are not interested in justice, they are interested in quiet.

—*Bill Cosby*

Children are natural mimics—they act like their parents in spite of our efforts to teach them good manners.

—*Anonymous*

In spite of the seven thousand books of
expert advice, the right way
to discipline a child is still a mystery to
most fathers and . . . mothers. Only
your grandmother and Ghengis Khan
know how to do it.

—*Bill Cosby*

I have found the best way to give advice to your children is to find out what they want and then advise them to do it.

—*Harry S. Truman*

Never raise your hand to your children; it leaves your midsection unprotected.

—*Robert Orben*

There are three ways to get something done: do it yourself, hire someone, or forbid your kids to do it.

—*Monta Crane*

An effective guilt tactic is suddenly to yell out, "I see you!" when your children are in a different room.

—*Bill Dodds*

Mother Nature is providential. She gives us twelve years to develop a love for our children before turning them into teenagers.

—*William Galvin*

It's amazing. One day you look at your phone bill and realize they're teenagers.

—*Milton Berle*

Between the ages of twelve and seventeen a parent can age thirty years.

—*Sam Levenson*

My little boys are growing up . . .
the baby's five-foot three!
It's great, but must they take such pride
in looking down on me?

—*Susan D. Anderson*

There used to be a saying that once your kid got old enough to help around the house, he was no longer around the house to help.

—*Theresa Bloomingdale*

No need to worry about your teenagers when they're not at home. A national survey revealed that they all go to the same place—"out"—and they all do the same thing—"nothing."

—*Bruce Lansky*

When the phone rings, it's for your teenager.
When the phone bill arrives, it's for you.

—*Bruce Lansky*

Puberty is the stage children reach that gets
parents to start worrying about pregnancy
all over again.

—*Joyce Armor*

One thing you can never find in a
teenager's room is the floor.

—*Bruce Lansky*

There is nothing wrong with teenagers that reasoning with them won't aggravate.

—*Anonymous*

Never lend your car to anyone to whom you have given birth.

—*Erma Bombeck*

If Abraham's son had been a teenager, it wouldn't have been a sacrifice.

—*Scott Spendlove*

When I was a boy of fourteen, my father was so ignorant I could hardly stand to have the old man around. But when I got to twenty-one, I was astonished at how much he had learned in seven years.

—*Mark Twain*

I have a daughter who goes to S.M.U. She could've gone to U.C.L.A. here in California, but it's got one more letter she'd have to remember.

—*Shecky Greene*

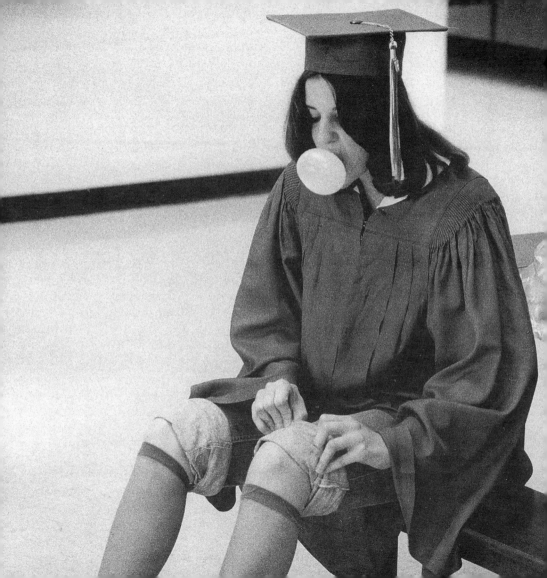

Much worse than rebellious teenagers are those who don't rebel and refuse to leave home.

—*Bruce Lansky*

I gave my son a hint. On his room door I put a sign: CHECKOUT TIME IS 18.

—*Milton Berle*

There isn't a child who hasn't gone out into the brave new world who eventually doesn't return to the old homestead carrying a bundle of dirty clothes.

—*Art Buchwald*

The bill from college came today
for all our children's fees;
as parents we are doomed to grow
much poorer by degrees.

—*Charles Ghigna*

A mother becomes a true grandmother the day she stops noticing the terrible things her children do because she is so enchanted with the wonderful things her grandchildren do.

—*Lois Wyse*

If your baby is "beautiful and perfect, never cries or fusses, sleeps on schedule and burps on demand, an angel all the time," you're the grandma.

—*Theresa Bloomingdale*

A grandmother will put a sweater on you
when she is cold, feed you when
she is hungry, and put you to bed when
she is tired.

—*Erma Bombeck*

Infant undershirts were made to keep
grandmothers happy on those chilly 90
degree days in mid August.

—*Linda Fiterman*

Grandma knows best,
but no one ever listens.

—*Mary McBride*

You feel completely comfortable entrusting your baby to [them] for long periods, which is why most grandparents flee to Florida at the earliest opportunity.

—*Dave Barry*

My parents have been visiting me for a few days. I just dropped them off at the airport. They leave tomorrow.

—*Margaret Smith*

Did you ever wonder how someone
who wasn't good enough for your
daughter could sire grandchildren who
were so brilliant and charming?

—Bruce Lansky

By the time the youngest children
have learned to keep the house tidy,
the oldest grandchildren are on hand
to tear it to pieces.

—Christopher Morley

If I had known grandchildren were so much fun, I'd have had them first.

—T-shirt

There's one thing about children—they never go around showing snapshots of their grandparents.

—Leopold Fechtner

The reason grandparents and grandchildren get along so well is that they have a common enemy.

—Sam Levenson

The good news is that grandchildren keep you young. The bad news is that after you spend time with them you feel your age.

—*Joan Holleman and Audrey Sherins*

Order Form

Qty.	Title	Author	Order No.	Unit Cost	Total
	Baby & Child Emergency First Aid	Einzig, M.	1380	$15.00	
	Baby & Child Medical Care	Hart, T.	1159	$8.00	
	Baby Journal	Bennett, M.	3172	$10.00	
	Baby Name Personality Survey	Lansky/Sinrod	1270	$7.00	
	Best Baby Name Book	Lansky, B.	1029	$5.00	
	Best Baby Shower Book	Cooke, C.	1239	$7.00	
	Dads Say the Dumbest Things!	Lansky/Jones	4220	$6.00	
	Discipline Without Shouting/Spanking	Wyckhoff/Unell	1079	$6.00	
	Feed Me! I'm Yours	Lansky, V.	1109	$8.00	
	First-Year Baby Care	Kelly, P.	1119	$7.00	
	Funny Side of Parenthood	Lansky, B.	4015	$6.00	
	Getting Organized for Your Baby	Bard, M.	1229	$5.00	
	Grandma Knows Best	McBride, M.	4009	$5.00	
	Joy of Parenthood	Blaustone, J.	3500	$6.00	
	Maternal Journal	Bennett, M.	3171	$10.00	
	Moms Say the Funniest Things!	Lansky, B.	4280	$6.00	
	Practical Parenting Tips	Lansky, V.	1180	$8.00	
				Subtotal	
			Shipping and Handling (see below)		
			MN residents add 6.5% sales tax		
				Total	

YES! Please send me the books indicated above. Add $2.00 shipping and handling for the first book and 50¢ for each additional book. Add $2.50 to total for books shipped to Canada. Overseas postage will be billed. Allow up to 4 weeks for delivery. Send check or money order payable to Meadowbrook Press. No cash or C.O.D's, please. Prices subject to change without notice. **Quantity discounts available upon request.**
Send book(s) to:

Name _____ Address _____

City _____ State _____ Zip _____ Telephone (____) _____

P.O. number (if necessary) _____ Payment via: ❑ Check or money order payable to Meadowbrook Press

Amount enclosed $ _____ ❑ Visa ❑ MasterCard (for orders over $10.00 only)

Account # _____ Signature _____ Exp. Date _____

A *FREE* Meadowbrook Press catalog is available upon request.

Mail to: Meadowbrook, Inc.
18318 Minnetonka Boulevard, Deephaven, MN 55391

(612) 473-5400   Toll-Free 1-800-338-2232   Fax (612) 475-0736